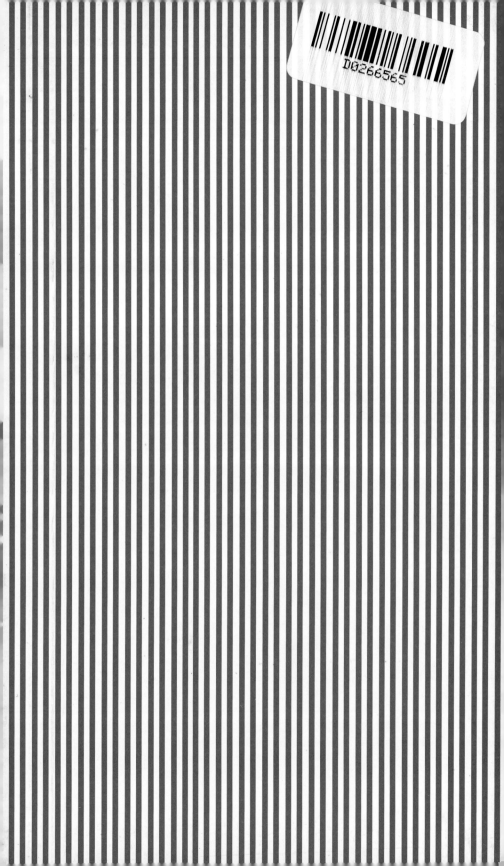

MAKE, BAKE, CUPCAKE

cupcake recipes and recollections

MAKE, BAKE, CUPCAKE

cupcake recipes and recollections

This edition published by Parragon Books Ltd in 2014

LOVE FOOD is an imprint of Parragon Books Ltd

Parragon Books Ltd
Chartist House
15–17 Trim Street
Bath, BA1 1HA, UK
www.parragon.com/lovefood

ISBN: 978-1-4723-3168-7

Printed in China

Designed by Amy Child
New text by Anne Sheasby
Illustrations by Charlotte Farmer

Notes for the Reader

This book uses both metric and imperial measurements. Follow the same units of measurement throughout; do not mix metric and imperial. All spoon measurements are level: teaspoons are assumed to be 5 ml, and tablespoons are assumed to be 15 ml. Unless otherwise stated, milk is assumed to be full fat, eggs and individual vegetables are medium, and pepper is freshly ground black pepper. Unless otherwise stated, all root vegetables should be peeled prior to using.

Garnishes, decorations and serving suggestions are all optional and not necessarily included in the recipe ingredients or method. The times given are an approximate guide only. Preparation times differ according to the techniques used by different people and the cooking times may also vary from those given. Optional ingredients, variations or serving suggestions have not been included in the time calculations.

Welcome to the wonderful world of cupcakes!

Cupcake lovers rejoice, there is now somewhere to jot down your thoughts and feelings about that most amazing of cakes, the cupcake! This is the perfect place to make notes about your favourite cupcake flavours, to plan out cupcake baking days, or just to jot down ideas for new cupcake recipes, the more wacky and out there the better! So join the cupcake revolution and enter a land where indulgent frosting and deliciously soft sponge rules....

Vanilla Cupcakes
The classic cupcake!

MAKES 12

175 g/6 oz unsalted
butter, softened
175 g/6 oz caster sugar
3 large eggs, beaten
1 tsp vanilla extract
175 g/6 oz self-raising
flour

FROSTING

150 g/5½ oz unsalted
butter, softened
3 tbsp double cream
or milk
1 tsp vanilla extract
300 g/10½ oz icing
sugar, sifted
hundreds and thousands,
to decorate

Step 1: Preheat the oven to 180°C/350°F/ Gas Mark 4. Place 12 paper cases in a muffin tin.

Step 2: Put the butter and caster sugar into a bowl and beat together until pale and creamy. Gradually beat in the eggs and vanilla extract. Sift in the flour and fold in gently.

Step 3: Divide the mixture evenly between the paper cases and bake in the preheated oven for 15–20 minutes, or until risen and firm to the touch. Transfer to a wire rack and leave to cool.

Step 4: To make the frosting, put the butter into a bowl and beat with an electric mixer for 2–3 minutes, or until pale and creamy. Beat in the cream and vanilla extract. Gradually beat in the icing sugar and continue beating until the buttercream is light and fluffy.

Step 5: Use a palette knife to swirl the frosting over the tops of the cupcakes. Decorate with hundreds and thousands.

Recipe Keeper

Recipe title ....

MAKES ....

INGREDIENTS:

....
....
....
....
....
....
....
....
....
....
....
....
....
....
....
....
....
....
....
....

STEPS:

....
....
....
....
....
....
....
....
....
....
....
....
....
....
....
....
....
....
....
....
....
....
....
....
....
....
....
....
....
....
....

Draw in your cupcake!

NOTES:

....
....
....
....
....
....
....
....
....
....
....
....
....

Shopping List

....

....

....

....

....

....

....

....

....

....

....

....

....

....

....

....

....

....

....

Don't
forget the
chocolate
sprinkles!

Design Your Own Cupcake!

Go wild with the glitter sprinkles!

Chocolate Cupcakes
For chocolate lovers!

MAKES 18

50 g/1¾ oz soft margarine

115 g/4 oz soft dark brown sugar

2 large eggs, beaten

115 g/4 oz plain flour

½ tsp bicarbonate of soda

25 g/1 oz cocoa powder

125 ml/4 fl oz soured cream

chocolate caraque, to decorate

FROSTING

125 g/4½ oz plain chocolate, broken into pieces

2 tbsp caster sugar

150 ml/5 fl oz soured cream

Step 1: Preheat the oven to 180°C/350°F/ Gas Mark 4. Place 18 paper cases in a bun tin.

Step 2: Put the margarine, brown sugar, eggs, flour, bicarbonate of soda and cocoa powder in a large bowl and beat together until just smooth. Using a metal spoon, fold in the soured cream. Divide the mixture evenly between the paper cases.

Step 3: Bake the cupcakes in the preheated oven for 20 minutes, or until well risen and firm to the touch. Transfer to a wire rack to cool.

Step 4: To make the frosting, put the chocolate into a heatproof bowl set over a saucepan of gently simmering water and heat until melted, stirring occasionally. Remove from the heat and allow to cool slightly, then whisk in the caster sugar and soured cream until combined. Spread the frosting over the tops of the cupcakes and leave to set in the refrigerator. Serve decorated with chocolate caraque.

My Favourite Cupcakes!

Fill out the names of your favourite bakeries and what flavour cupcakes you like to buy there!

Bakery:

My favourite flavours are:

Bakery:

My favourite flavours are:

Bakery:

My favourite flavours are:

Bakery:

My favourite flavours are:

Bakery:

My favourite flavours are:

Bakery:

My favourite flavours are:

Bakery:

My favourite flavours are:

Bakery:

My favourite flavours are:

Bakery:

My favourite flavours are:

Bakery:

My favourite flavours are:

Indulgence Day Cupcakes!

For days when you just don't care about the calories, try these!

Double Chocolate Cupcakes with Fudge Frosting

White Chocolate & Rum Cupcakes with Vanilla Buttercream

Mocha Cupcakes with Chocolate Frosting & Sprinkles

Chocolate Chip Cupcakes with Royal Icing

What are your favourite indulgence day cupcakes?

....

....

....

....

....

....

....

Skinny Day Cupcakes!

On days when you feel good and virtuous, try these!

Mixed Berry Cupcakes

Carrot Cake Cupcakes

Lemon Drizzle Cupcakes

Beetroot Cupcakes with Vegan Chocolate Icing

What are your favourite skinny day cupcakes?

....

....

....

....

....

....

....

My Recipe Ideas

Use your imagination to come up with some new cupcake recipe ideas!

Red Velvet Cupcakes
Gorgeously tasty!

MAKES 12

140 g/5 oz plain flour

1 tsp bicarbonate of soda

2 tbsp cocoa powder

115 g/4 oz butter, softened

140 g/5 oz caster sugar

1 large egg, beaten

125 ml/4 fl oz buttermilk

1 tsp vanilla extract

1 tbsp red food colouring

red coloured sugar or red sugar sprinkles, to decorate

FROSTING

140 g/5 oz full-fat soft cheese

85 g/3 oz unsalted butter, softened

280 g/10 oz icing sugar, sifted

Step 1: Preheat the oven to 180°C/350°F/ Gas Mark 4. Put 12 paper cases in a bun tin.

Step 2: Sift together the flour, bicarbonate of soda and cocoa powder. Place the butter and sugar in a bowl and beat together until pale and creamy. Gradually beat in the egg and half the flour mixture. Beat in the buttermilk, vanilla extract and food colouring. Fold in the remaining flour mixture. Divide the mixture evenly between the paper cases.

Step 3: Bake the cupcakes in the preheated oven for 15–20 minutes, or until risen and firm to the touch. Transfer to a wire rack and leave to cool.

Step 4: To make the frosting, put the soft cheese and butter in a bowl and blend together with a spatula. Beat in the icing sugar until smooth and creamy. Swirl the frosting on the top of the cupcakes. Sprinkle with the red sugar.

A Cupcake for

Spring

Bake Easter Spice Cupcakes?

....
....
....
....
....
....
....

Summer

Bake Ice Cream Sundae Cupcakes?

....
....
....
....
....
....
....

All Seasons

Autumn

Bake Apple
Crumble
Cupcakes?

....
....
....
....
....
....

Winter

Bake Christmas
Holly Cupcakes?

....
....
....
....
....
....

Cupcakes are fairy cakes with attitude!

Eat a balanced diet, a cupcake in each hand!

Keep calm and bake cupcakes!

When life gives you lemons, bake Lemon Drizzle Cupcakes!

Cocktails & Cupcakes

What could go better with a delicious cupcake than a fabulously decadent cocktail? Think of some cupcakes you could bake to go with these wonderful cocktails...

Cosmopolitan

Cranberry
Cupcakes

Tequila
Sunrise

Chocolate Orange
Cupcakes

Pina Colada

....

....

Moscow Mule

....

....

Raspberry Daiquiri

....

....

Mai Tai

....

....

Buck's Fizz

....

....

Woo-Woo

....

....

Frosted Berry Cupcakes

Perfect for summer!

MAKES 12

115 g/4 oz butter, softened, or soft margarine
115 g/4 oz caster sugar
2 tsp orange flower water
2 large eggs, beaten
55 g/2 oz ground almonds
115 g/4 oz self-raising flour
2 tbsp milk

FROSTING

300 g/10½ oz mascarpone cheese
85 g/3 oz caster sugar
4 tbsp orange juice

DECORATION

280 g/10 oz berries
fresh mint leaves
egg white
sugar

Step 1: Preheat the oven to 180°C/350°F/Gas Mark 4. Place 12 paper cases in a bun tin.

Step 2: Place the butter, caster sugar and orange flower water in a large bowl and beat together until light and fluffy. Gradually beat in the eggs. Stir in the ground almonds. Sift in the flour and, using a metal spoon, fold in gently with the milk.

Step 3: Divide the mixture evenly between the paper cases. Bake in the preheated oven for 15–20 minutes, or until risen, golden and firm to the touch. Transfer to a wire rack and leave to cool.

Step 4: To make the frosting, put the mascarpone, caster sugar and orange juice in a bowl and beat together until smooth.

Step 5: Swirl the frosting over the top of the cupcakes. Brush the berries and mint leaves with egg white and roll in the sugar to coat. Decorate the cupcakes with the frosted berries and leaves.

Recipe Keeper

Recipe title ....

MAKES ....

INGREDIENTS:

....
....
....
....
....
....
....
....
....
....
....
....
....
....
....
....
....
....
....
....
....
....

STEPS:

....
....
....
....
....
....
....
....
....
....
....
....
....
....
....
....
....
....
....
....
....
....
....
....
....
....
....
....
....
....
....
....
....
....
....

Draw in your cupcake!

NOTES:

....
....
....
....
....
....
....
....
....
....
....
....

Shopping List

Don't forget the pink glitter!

The Story of the Cupcake

The whole world has gone cupcake crazy over the past few years, but did you know that cupcakes date back as far as the 18th century? The first ever recorded mention of cupcakes was in a baking book from 1796, where it refers to a 'cake to be baked in small cups'. Or, as we would now call it, cupcakes! During the 19th century, cupcakes started to be regularly cooked in small cups or ramekins, which is how the cupcake got its official name. In the 20th century, cupcakes were also known as fairy cakes or patty cakes, but as cupcakes have become increasingly popular in the 21st century, this name has stuck and cupcakes now reign supreme!

Pineapple Cupcakes
Tropical flavours!

MAKES 12

115 g/4 oz unsalted butter, softened

115 g/4 oz caster sugar

2 eggs, beaten

115 g/4 oz self-raising flour

3 canned pineapple rings, drained and finely chopped

FROSTING

115 g/4 oz unsalted butter, softened

115 g/4 oz full-fat soft cheese

280 g/10 oz icing sugar, sifted

55 g/2 oz desiccated coconut

25 g/1 oz glacé pineapple, chopped, to decorate

Step 1: Preheat the oven to 180°C/350°F/ Gas Mark 4. Place 12 paper cases in a bun tin.

Step 2: Put the butter and caster sugar into a bowl and beat together until pale and creamy. Gradually beat in the eggs. Sift in the flour and fold in gently. Fold in the chopped pineapple.

Step 3: Divide the mixture evenly between the paper cases and bake in the preheated oven for 15–20 minutes, or until risen and firm to the touch. Transfer to a wire rack and leave to cool.

Step 4: To make the frosting, beat together the butter and soft cheese until smooth. Gradually beat in the icing sugar, then fold in the coconut.

Step 5: Swirl the frosting over the tops of the cupcakes and decorate with the glacé pineapple.

Top Tips for Perfect Cupcakes

Write down any top tips that you discover when baking cupcakes!

....
....
....
....
....
....
....
....
....
....
....
....
....
....

Bling it Up!

There is nothing more satisfying than turning an average-looking cupcake into a beautifully decorated work of genius! Here are some ways to decorate your cupcakes – why not add some of your own?

Scatter over some sugar sprinkles, they come in all colours!

Treat the person in your life to a cupcake scattered with rose petals.

Try adding bling with glimmer sugar.

Make a cupcake fit for a disco diva with edible glitter.

Fresh berries add a colourful and more healthy touch!

Little sweets on the top of a cupcake are so cute!

My Cupcake Memories!

Cupcakes evoke so many happy memories – record some of your favourite recollections here....

Cherry Sundae Cupcakes

Something extra special!

MAKES 12

175 g/6 oz butter, softened, or soft margarine

175 g/6 oz caster sugar

3 eggs, beaten

1 tsp vanilla extract

200 g/7 oz plain flour

1½ tsp baking powder

55 g/2 oz glacé cherries, chopped

CHOCOLATE SAUCE

85 g/3 oz plain chocolate, broken into pieces

25 g/1 oz butter

1 tbsp golden syrup

DECORATION

600 ml/1 pint double cream

2 tbsp toasted chopped mixed nuts

pink glimmer sugar

12 maraschino cherries

Step 1: Preheat the oven to 160°C/325°F/Gas Mark 3. Place 12 paper cases in a muffin tin.

Step 2: Place the butter and caster sugar in a large bowl and beat together until light and fluffy. Gradually beat in the eggs and vanilla extract. Sift in the flour and baking powder and, using a metal spoon, fold in gently. Fold in the glacé cherries.

Step 3: Divide the mixture evenly between the paper cases. Bake in the preheated oven for 25–30 minutes, or until risen, golden and firm to the touch. Transfer to a wire rack and leave to cool.

Step 4: To make the chocolate sauce, place the chocolate, butter and syrup in a heatproof bowl set over a saucepan of simmering water and heat until melted. Remove from the heat and stir until smooth. Leave to cool, stirring occasionally, for 20–30 minutes.

Step 5: Whip the cream until holding firm peaks. Spoon into a piping bag fitted with a large star nozzle and pipe large swirls of cream on top of each cupcake. Drizzle over the chocolate sauce and sprinkle with the chopped nuts and pink sugar. Top each with a maraschino cherry.

A Cupcake for Every Day of the Week!

It's important to stay on top of your diary – why not make a start by planning which cupcakes to eat this week?

Monday   Tuesday   Wednesday

Need a pick-me-up – it's got to be Double Chocolate Cupcakes!

Thursday

Friday

Saturday &
Sunday

Meeting the
girls at the
café – try the
new Mojito
Cupcake?

You are the frosting to my cupcake.

Make cupcakes not war!

Never mind the chicken soup, my soul needs cupcakes!

All you need is a large cupcake, and someone to share it with.

Make Sure You Get

Raspberry
Cupcake

Spiced Carrot
Cupcake

Your Five a Day!

Apple Streusel Cupcake

Berry Cupcake

Strawberries & Cream Cupcake

White Chocolate & Rose Cupcakes

Great as a romantic gift!

MAKES 12

115 g/4 oz unsalted butter, softened

115 g/4 oz caster sugar

1 tsp rosewater

2 eggs, beaten

115 g/4 oz self-raising flour

55 g/2 oz white chocolate, grated

sugar-frosted pink rose petals, to decorate

FROSTING

115 g/4 oz white chocolate, broken into pieces

2 tbsp milk

175 g/6 oz full-fat soft cheese

25 g/1 oz icing sugar, sifted

Step 1: Preheat the oven to 180°C/350°F/ Gas Mark 4. Place 12 paper cases in a bun tin.

Step 2: Place the butter, sugar and rosewater in a bowl and beat together until pale and creamy. Gradually beat in the eggs. Sift over the flour and fold in gently. Fold in the white chocolate. Divide the mixture evenly between the paper cases.

Step 3: Bake the cupcakes in the preheated oven for 15–20 minutes, or until risen, golden and firm to the touch. Transfer the cupcakes to a wire rack and leave to cool.

Step 4: To make the frosting, place the chocolate and milk in a heatproof bowl set over a saucepan of simmering water and heat until melted. Remove from the heat and stir until smooth. Cool for 30 minutes. Put the soft cheese and icing sugar in a bowl and beat together until smooth and creamy. Fold in the chocolate. Chill in the refrigerator for 1 hour. Swirl the frosting over the top of the cupcakes. Decorate with the sugar-frosted rose petals.

Rainy Day Cupcakes

A rainy day is the perfect day to bake! Take advantage of staying in and think of some cupcake baking challenges....

1. Try making my own royal icing...

2. Decorate cupcakes for a Halloween party — try making zombie cupcakes!.....

Recipe Keeper

Recipe title ....

MAKES ....

INGREDIENTS:

....
....
....
....
....
....
....
....
....
....
....
....
....
....
....
....
....
....
....
....

STEPS:

....
....
....
....
....
....
....
....
....
....
....
....
....
....
....
....
....
....
....
....
....
....
....
....
....
....
....
....
....
....
....
....
....
....
....
....
....

Draw in your cupcake!

NOTES:

....
....
....
....
....
....
....
....
....
....
....
....
....

Shopping List

Don't forget the fondant icing!

Apple Streusel Cupcakes
A taste of autumn!

MAKES 14

½ tsp bicarbonate of soda
280 g/10 oz apple sauce (from a jar)
55 g/2 oz butter, softened, or soft margarine
85 g/3 oz demerara sugar
1 large egg, beaten
175 g/6 oz self-raising flour
½ tsp ground cinnamon
½ tsp freshly grated nutmeg

TOPPING

50 g/1¾ oz plain flour
50 g/1¾ oz demerara sugar
¼ tsp ground cinnamon
¼ tsp freshly grated nutmeg
35 g/1¼ oz butter, softened

Step 1: Preheat the oven to 180°C/350°F/Gas Mark 4. Place 14 paper cases in a bun tin.

Step 2: To make the topping, put the flour, demerara sugar, cinnamon and nutmeg in a bowl. Cut the butter into small pieces, then add to the bowl and rub it in with your fingertips until the mixture resembles fine breadcrumbs.

Step 3: Add the bicarbonate of soda to the apple sauce and stir until dissolved. Place the butter and demerara sugar in a large bowl and beat together until pale and creamy. Gradually beat in the egg. Sift in the flour, cinnamon and nutmeg and, using a metal spoon, fold into the mixture, alternating with the apple sauce mixture.

Step 4: Divide the mixture evenly between the paper cases. Scatter the topping over the cupcakes and press down gently. Bake in the preheated oven for 20 minutes, or until risen, golden and firm to the touch. Transfer to a wire rack and leave to cool.

The Skinny on Cupcakes!

There are NATIONAL CUPCAKE DAYS and even NATIONAL CUPCAKE WEEKS in many countries all over the world. There is no official day worldwide and it varies from country to country!

One of the STRANGEST cupcakes ever made was the cupcake car! Designed in the shape of a cupcake in 2009, this US-made car could travel up to 7 mph and was priced at $25,000!

There are a variety of COMPETITIVE EATING contests especially for cupcakes! These include the contests for eating the most cupcakes overall, as well as timed races for eating the most within a certain timescale.

There are some STRANGE CUPCAKE FLAVOURS out there! Who fancies trying Maple & Bacon, Mango & Chilli, or Meatloaf with Mashed Potato Icing Cupcakes?

One of the world's MOST EXPENSIVE CUPCAKES ever was the $55,000 Red Velvet Cupcake from America – it came baked with an 8-carat diamond engagement ring inside it!

Design Your Own Cupcake!

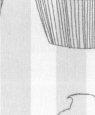

Apply some glimmer sugar!

Decorate with Love

Make a cupcake for someone you love! Why not try these romantic decorating ideas?

Cut some hearts from red fondant icing and place in the buttercream frosting.

Buy some sugar roses and place them on top of your partner's favourite frosted cupcake.

Place a red ribbon around a cupcake box and tie with a pretty bow.

Scatter some sugar-frosted rose petals on top of Red Velvet Cupcakes.

Coffee Cupcakes
A great start to the morning!

MAKES 12

115 g/4 oz unsalted butter, softened

115 g/4 oz soft light brown sugar

2 eggs, beaten

115 g/4 oz self-raising flour, sifted

½ tsp baking powder

2 tsp coffee granules

25 g/1 oz icing sugar

4 tbsp water

2 tbsp finely grated plain chocolate, for dusting

FROSTING

225 g/8 oz mascarpone cheese

85 g/3 oz caster sugar

2 tbsp Marsala or sweet sherry

Step 1: Preheat the oven to 180°C/350°F/ Gas Mark 4. Place 12 paper cases in a bun tin.

Step 2: Place the butter, brown sugar, eggs, flour and baking powder in a bowl and beat together until pale and creamy. Divide the mixture evenly between the paper cases.

Step 3: Bake the cupcakes in the preheated oven for 15–20 minutes, or until risen, golden and firm to the touch.

Step 4: Place the coffee granules, icing sugar and water in a saucepan and heat gently, stirring, until the coffee and sugar have dissolved. Boil for 1 minute then leave to cool for 10 minutes. Brush the coffee syrup over the top of the warm cupcakes. Transfer the cupcakes to a wire rack and leave to cool.

Step 5: For the frosting, put the mascarpone, sugar and Marsala in a bowl and beat together until smooth. Spread over the top of the cakes. Using a star template, sprinkle the grated chocolate over the frosting.

Happy Cupcake Day!

It's just one of those baking days where everything goes right!

The tops have peaked perfectly!

All a lovely even colour!

Wonderfully crisp on top!

Bad Cupcake Day!

It's a disaster!

The bottoms have burnt!

I forgot to put in the sugar!

The Cupcakes I've Baked

Cupcake baked:	My thoughts:

Friend & family comments:

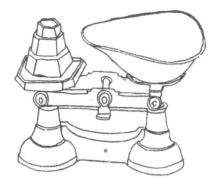

The Rise of the Cupcake

The cult of the cupcake has been on the rise over the last two decades and the craze currently shows no signs of stopping! Since the 1990s, cupcakes have been everywhere, with specialist bakeries springing up in most town centres to cupcakes making an appearance on the TV show 'Sex and the City' in 2000. Their popularity has been explained as nostalgia for the cakes of the past or because they symbolize femininity and friendship. Whatever the reason, cupcakes are now part of our culinary landscape and are here to stay! Amen to that!

Candy Store Cupcakes
Fun treats!

MAKES 12

150 g/5½ oz butter, softened, or soft margarine

150 g/5½ oz caster sugar

3 eggs, beaten

150 g/5½ oz self-raising flour

4 tsp strawberry flavoured popping candy

sweets of your choice, to decorate (optional)

BUTTERCREAM

175 g/6 oz unsalted butter, softened

2 tbsp milk

350 g/12 oz icing sugar

pink and yellow food colourings

Step 1: Preheat the oven to 180°C/350°F/ Gas Mark 4. Place 12 paper cases in a bun tin.

Step 2: Place the butter and caster sugar in a large bowl and beat together until pale and creamy. Gradually beat in the eggs. Sift in the flour and, using a metal spoon, fold in gently. Fold in half of the popping candy.

Step 3: Divide the mixture evenly between the paper cases. Bake in the preheated oven for 18–22 minutes, or until risen, golden and firm to the touch. Transfer to a wire rack and leave to cool.

Step 4: To make the buttercream, place the butter in a bowl and beat until pale and creamy. Beat in the milk, then gradually sift in the icing sugar and continue beating for 2–3 minutes, or until the buttercream is light and fluffy. Divide the buttercream between two bowls and beat a little pink or yellow food colouring into each bowl.

Step 5: Pipe or swirl the buttercream on top of the cupcakes and decorate with sweets, if using. Sprinkle over the remaining popping candy just before serving.

Recipe Keeper

Recipe title ....

MAKES .... STEPS:

INGREDIENTS:

Draw in your cupcake!

NOTES:

....
....
....
....
....
....
....
....
....
....
....
....

Shopping List

Don't
forget the
gold
ribbon!

Cute Presentation Ideas

Place your cupcakes on a pretty cupcake stand!

A cellophane bag is a perfect way to present a single cupcake as a gift.

Put your cupcakes into a presentation box — some include special inserts to keep your cupcakes in place.

Placing a cupcake wrapper around each cupcake instantly adds a decorated look to your bakes.

Adding a ribbon to a cupcake box or cellophane bag finishes the look off perfectly.

Displaying your cupcakes on vintage crockery gives them a fabulously retro look!

Banana & Pecan Cupcakes

Gorgeous nutty flavour!

MAKES 24

115 g/4 oz butter, softened, or soft margarine

115 g/4 oz caster sugar

½ tsp vanilla extract

2 eggs, lightly beaten

2 ripe bananas, mashed

4 tbsp soured cream

225 g/8 oz plain flour

1¼ tsp baking powder

¼ tsp bicarbonate of soda

55 g/2 oz pecan nuts, roughly chopped

24 pecan nut halves, to decorate

BUTTERCREAM

115 g/4 oz unsalted butter, softened

175 g/6 oz icing sugar

Step 1: Preheat the oven to 190°C/375°F/ Gas Mark 5. Put 24 paper cases in bun tins.

Step 2: Place the butter, caster sugar and vanilla extract in a large bowl and beat together until light and fluffy. Gradually beat in the eggs. Stir in the mashed bananas and soured cream. Sift in the flour, baking powder and bicarbonate of soda and, using a metal spoon, fold into the mixture with the chopped pecan nuts.

Step 3: Spoon the mixture into the paper cases. Bake in the preheated oven for 20 minutes, or until risen, golden and firm to the touch. Transfer to a wire rack and leave to cool.

Step 4: To make the buttercream, put the butter in a bowl and beat until fluffy. Sift in the icing sugar and mix together well.

Step 5: Spoon the buttercream into a large piping bag fitted with a large star nozzle. Pipe a swirl of buttercream on top of each cupcake and decorate with a pecan nut half.

Cupcake Bakery

Think of fun names for when you open your own cupcake bakery!

....

....

....

....

....

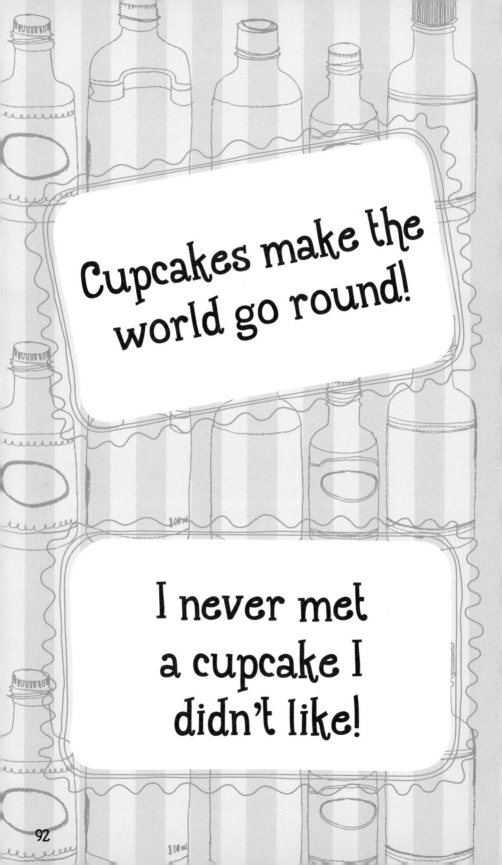

Cupcakes make the world go round!

I never met a cupcake I didn't like!

There's no such thing as too many cupcakes....

Bake a cupcake, share the love.

My Friends' Favourite Cupcakes

Friend:

Their favourite flavour:

Friend:	Their favourite flavour:

Pink Lemonade Cupcakes

Fun and fresh!

MAKES 10

115 g/4 oz self-raising flour

¼ tsp baking powder

115 g/4 oz butter, softened, or soft margarine

115 g/4 oz caster sugar

2 large eggs, lightly beaten

pink food colouring

55 g/2 oz granulated sugar

juice of 1 small lemon

BUTTERCREAM

115 g/4 oz unsalted butter, softened

juice and finely grated rind of ½ lemon

4 tbsp double cream

225 g/8 oz icing sugar

pink food colouring

TO DECORATE

pink and white sugar sprinkles

pink, white and red hundreds and thousands

10 pink or yellow drinking straws, cut into 8-cm/3-inch lengths

Step 1: Preheat the oven to 180°C/350°F/Gas Mark 4. Put 10 paper cases in a bun tin.

Step 2: Sift the flour and baking powder into a large bowl. Add the butter, caster sugar and eggs and beat together until smooth. Beat in a little pink food colouring to colour the mixture pale pink. Spoon the mixture into the paper cases. Bake in the preheated oven for 15–20 minutes, until risen and firm to the touch.

Step 3: Meanwhile, place the granulated sugar and lemon juice in a saucepan and heat gently until the sugar has dissolved. Leave to cool. Prick the cake tops with a skewer and brush with the lemon syrup. Transfer to a wire rack and leave to cool.

Step 4: To make the buttercream, place the butter, lemon juice and lemon rind in a bowl and beat for 2–3 minutes, until pale and creamy. Beat in the cream, then sift in the icing sugar and continue beating for 2–3 minutes, until the buttercream is fluffy. Beat in a little pink food colouring to give a pale pink colour.

Step 5: Swirl the buttercream over the cupcakes. Scatter sprinkles in the centre of 5 cupcakes and edge the other cupcakes with hundreds and thousands. Push the straws into the cupcakes.

Any Excuse for a Cupcake!

I'm a professional cupcake tester!

Well, you can't just have one cupcake....

I need to keep my blood sugar levels up!

My Recipe Ideas

Use your imagination to come up
with some new cupcake recipe ideas!

....
....
....
....
....
....
....
....
....
....
....
....
....
....
....
....

Your Dream Cupcake Box

Create your dream cupcake boxes by writing in your favourite flavour combinations here!

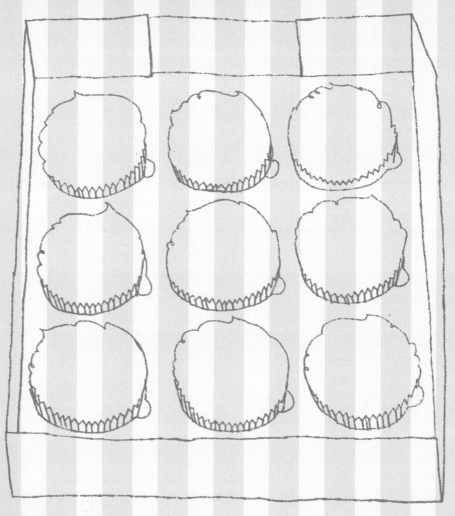

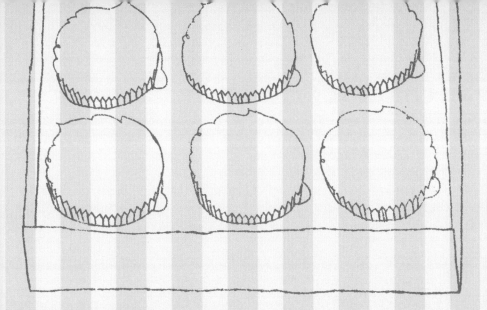

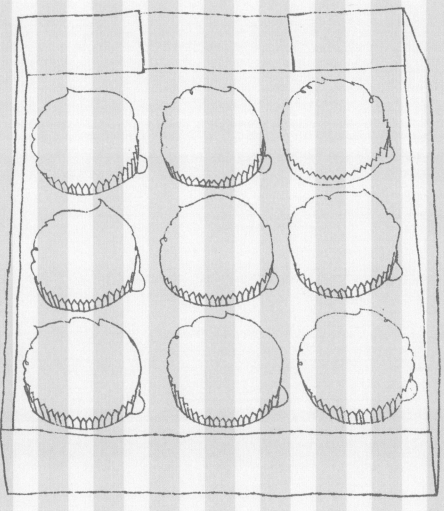

103

Buttercream Frosting
The icing on the cake!

MAKES 250 g/9 oz

100 g/3½ oz unsalted
butter, softened
150 g/5½ oz icing sugar
1 tbsp hot water

Step 1: Put the butter in a mixing bowl and beat with an electric mixer to soften. Add the icing sugar and beat well until smooth and creamy.

Step 2: Add the hot water and beat again until very soft and fluffy in texture.

Flavour variations:

Lemon – use 2 tbsp lemon juice instead of the water and add the finely grated rind of 1 lemon.

Orange – use 2 tbsp orange juice instead of the water and add the finely grated rind of 1 small orange.

Chocolate – blend 25 g/1 oz cocoa powder with 2 tbsp boiling water to make a paste. Add to the buttercream with 2 tsp vanilla extract and beat until smooth and creamy.

Lazy Cupcake Day!

Think of some quick and easy cupcakes you could bake today!

....

....

....

....

....

....

....

....

....

....

....

....

....

....

....

....

Cupcake Day Challenge!

Think of some challenging cupcakes you could bake today!

1.5kg

My Favourite Cookery Shows

Note down when your favourite cookery TV shows are on!

Monday   Tuesday   Wednesday

Thursday

Friday

Saturday &
Sunday

Cream Cheese Frosting

An American classic!

MAKES 250 g/9 oz

100 g/3½ oz full-fat
cream cheese
50 g/1¾ oz unsalted
butter, softened
1 tsp lemon juice
100 g/3½ oz icing sugar

Step 1: Beat together the cream cheese and butter with an electric mixer until smooth.

Step 2: Add the lemon juice and icing sugar and beat again until the frosting is light and creamy.

Recipe Keeper

Recipe title ....

MAKES ....

INGREDIENTS:

....
....
....
....
....
....
....
....
....
....
....
....
....
....
....
....
....
....
....

STEPS:

....
....
....
....
....
....
....
....
....
....
....
....
....
....
....
....
....
....
....
....
....
....
....
....
....
....
....
....
....
....
....
....
....
....
....

Draw in your cupcake!

NOTES:

....
....
....
....
....
....
....
....
....
....
....
....
....
....

Shopping List

Don't forget the caster sugar!

Burn it Off!

The average chocolate-frosted cupcake is around 400 calories – see how much exercise you would have to do to burn it off!

Activity:	Calories burnt per hour:
Stretching	180 calories
Walking	280 calories
Bicycling	290 calories
Dancing	330 calories
Hiking	370 calories
Gym workout	440 calories
Fast walking	460 calories
Aerobics	480 calories
Swimming	510 calories
Jogging	590 calories

Dark Chocolate Ganache
A luxurious topping!

MAKES 500 g/1 lb 2 oz

250 g/9 oz plain chocolate, chopped

250 ml/9 fl oz double cream

2 tbsp icing sugar

Step 1: Put the chocolate in a bowl. Heat the cream and sugar in a saucepan until beginning to bubble around the edges (but not boiling) and pour over the chocolate.

Step 2: Leave to stand, stirring frequently until the chocolate has melted and the ganache is smooth and glossy. It can be used as soon as it's cool enough to hold its shape.

Flavour variations:

For white chocolate ganache, use the same quantities as dark, but heat only half the cream to pour over the white chocolate. Once the chocolate has melted and the mixture is completely cold, stir in the remaining cream. Whisk lightly with an electric mixer until the ganache just holds its shape. Do not over-mix or the texture will be spoiled.

My Cupcake Triumphs

Even bake
on whole
batch!

My Cupcake Disasters

Ended up
with burnt
bottoms!

Throw a Cupcake Party!

Here are some ideas to get your cupcake party started!

Design your own cupcake-shaped invitations!

Have a theme, such as Zombie Cupcakes!

Make some booze-infused cupcakes to go with cocktails!

Hold a 'Best Cupcake' competition.

Make a horrible-tasting cupcake and play cupcake roulette!

Play some cupcake decorating games.

And it's time to say goodbye to the world of cupcakes.... But don't worry – you now have plenty of ideas for ways to fill your life with cupcakes, from baking delicious recipes through to fun ideas for decorating or even holding your own cupcake party! Embrace the wonderful world of cupcakes and let the baking revolution commence....